I0437594

Depths of Colour Psychology

Business Success and Personal Development

by
Reena Begum

authorHOUSE®

AuthorHouse™ UK Ltd.
500 Avebury Boulevard
Central Milton Keynes, MK9 2BE
www.authorhouse.co.uk
Phone: 08001974150

First published by AuthorHouse 4/8/2008

ISBN: 978-1-4343-6701-3 (sc)

Printed in the United States of America
Bloomington, Indiana

This book is printed on acid-free paper.

-Acknowledgement-

This book would not be what is without the constant love and support of my parents, my father (Ishad Ali), my mother (Moyjun N. Khanom) my sisters (Henara, Neena, Leena and Rubina), my brother (Md. Zia), and my nephew (Abdul Kalam), my Niece (Reshmi Begum).

I would also like to take this opportunity to thank Dr. Nigel Marlow, for contributing to this book with his three lively chapters, as well as thanking Master Tomas Coxon for his wise insights into Feng Shui. Further I would like to thank AuthorHouse for their anticipation and the assistant they have provided me to put my voice in print (so thank you to Caroline Haywood, Daniel Cooke, and the rest of the team).

And, finally thank you to all friends and family that I have to mentioned solely here. I really hope you enjoy reading this as much as I enjoyed writing it.

-Reena Begum-

1

What's in a name? Colour plays a vital element in the way we feel, think and behave. Often we assume certain factors to our emotions, and with the right or wrong colour we project various stimuli's. Businesses investing millions into employee productivity can have its ups and downs. Several questions may be lurking in your mind...

Figure 1.1 a diagram of the human mind and the questions many employers and employees project

This chapter looks into colour and how its applications can be used in work and home lives. The relationship between the individual and their mind. It has often led me to wonder why study colour? What is the significance of colour and its impact on us? So, I began to look at the current and existing literature on colour, and surprisingly, stumbled across environmental psychology, which in effect offers basis for analysing an individual's behaviour.

Within the context of environmental psychology there are may sub themes that have been critically examined by various theorists. Figure 1.2 is an extract from Gifford (1997), which provides a comprehensive overview of environmental psychology. Once the individual is in the environment; transacting with it consciously or not, the person thinks, feels, and behaves. These transactions often have important outcomes both for the person and the environment. Some outcomes are immediate and others are delayed.

Figure 1.2 diagram taken from Gifford (1997) reflecting the individual placed in the environment

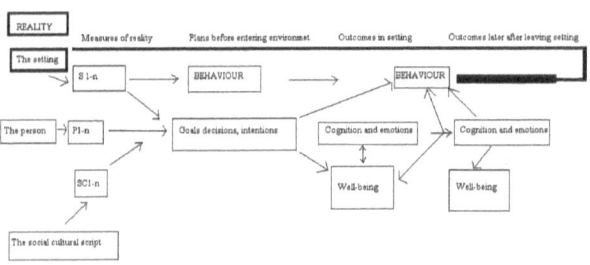

In comparison, Saegert (1993) developed a model, which explores the emotional responses derived from the environment. In this case being the settings. Figure 1.3 illustrates the diagram recording an individual's emotional arousal when placed in a particular setting.

Figure 1.3 an illustration of Saegert's model (1993) and levels of arousal

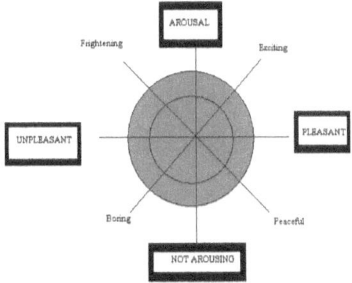

Figure 1.3 indicates two major dimensions of emotions and their hybrids that form a circumplex. Imagine your emotions are induced by the setting you are in right now, where would they be? Where would you fit them in the circumplex.

Two particular theorists in the field of measuring emotions are Russell and Mehrabian (1974); their notion of emotion was that it plays the part as a mediator between environment and personality (pre-existing influences and behaviours) as the outcomes.

Originally, their research identified three primary emotional responses: pleasure, arousal and dominance.

Later, however, Russell's (1980) research led him to conclude that dominance plays a poor third as a primary emotion, and therefore only pleasure and arousal are to be the primary emotions, and thus are viewed as being independent from one another.

As mentioned above, the environment plays a large part as to how we behave, feel or think. We often, if not most of the time (See Chapter 5-"A colourful Life") associate colours. If like me you always want to know where such "things" root from, you'd continue to read on.

Here is an insight of how colour is not just "colour" so to speak. Colour dates back as early as 129AD, when the Greek-Roman scholar Galen used colour classification to view existence in a more symbolically light. Thus, history recalls that there has never been a time when colour did not fascinate humanity and it has always been regarded as one of life's mysteries. Every civilisation had and even today associated itself with colour, but oddly enough none of them had or have named many colours.

Anthropologists Berlin & Kay (1960) conducted a worldwide study of colour naming, the study is not obtainable for further discussion. However, Aristotle (14th Century BC) considered the colours blue and yellow to be true primary colours, relating as they do life's polarities: Sun and Moon, male and female, stimulus and sedation, expansion and contraction, in and out.

Swiftly moving to the environment once again, one particular interesting point to consider; especially for businesses investing millions of pounds in interior design and offices; it would be wise to understand that environmental psychology is without a doubt a counterpart to office interiors.

Professor Sune Lindstrom cited in Mahnke, 1996, once said:

"With every particular architectural product is the spontaneous emotional reaction that is of importance."

Mahnke, 1990, himself conducted a study on human needs and illustrated the "Colour Experience" pyramid. Figure 1.4 illustrates our survival and basic needs associated to colours. May also play significant comparison to Maslow's Hierarchy of Needs.

Figure 1.4 an illustration of Mahnke's model (1990) based on the "Colour Experience" pyramid

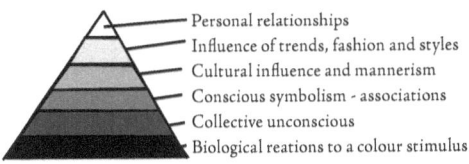

The "Colour Experience" pyramid provides an important understanding that we as human beings may be considered as having total colour vision, which must mean that the total spectrum is necessary for our survival biologically.

The "collective unconscious" labelled as the fifth element of the pyramid is seen as the part that is not controlled or caused by the intellect or conscious rational thoughts. According to Jungian psychology, the "collective unconscious" is the part of our psyche that has nothing to with conscious or unconscious reactions based on personal experience during our lifetime.

With regard to what has been mentioned above, the forth-level known as "conscious symbolism" also has significance, as it is believed to be an associative power of colour. Colour association (also know as "conscious symbolism") and their symbolic content is of importance to various fields such as fashion, advertising, product and graphic design. And thus, the symbolism of colour has always played a vital part in human life throughout history.

None the less, there have been many approaches to the study of both colour and its acquaintance to emotions. What is of substantial interest is that both Kobayashi and Mahnke have carried out research on colour. Taking both approaches (Kobayashi and Mahnke) it can be said that they are similar to that of Russell's Circumplex Model of Affect.

Figure 1.5 illustrates Kobayashi's analysis of colour; figure1.6 illustrates Mahnke's study of colour and interior design and; figure 1.7 illustrates Russell's structure of Affect

Figure 1.5

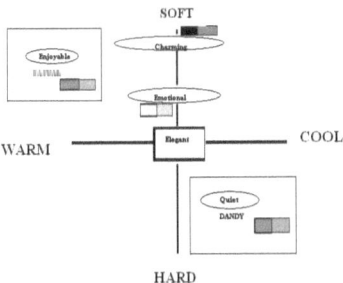

Figure 1.6

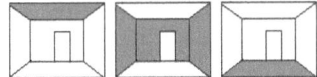

Figure 1.7

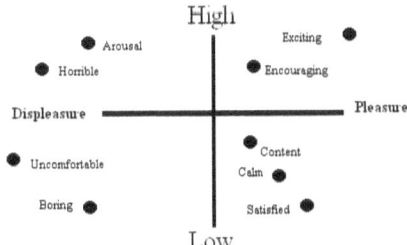

What is worth noting here is that Mahnke's diagram describes how a colour will influence the room's character differently depending on whether it is located on the ceiling, walls or floor.

A further look into the depths of colour lets on indulge into the associated factors. Such factors are our human senses, the five senses that we humans have a privilege to: Vision (Seeing), hearing, touch, smell and taste. We often more than other senses associate with the sense of vision.

Colour, more than anything else is has always been pretty much under studied, however, that's where it becomes interesting, the perception of noise and sound plays an integral part to how we sense colour. Gestalt Psychologists, Heinz Werner, Krakov, Allen and Swartz cited in Birren (1982), found that loud noises, strong odours and strong tastes make the eye more sensitive to green and less sensitive to red. For interior design purposes, often designers may profit from the relationship between noise and colour, which is believed to be more in the nature of mental associations.

Frieling, Director of the Institute of Colour Psychology found that stimulation of the senses, brightness and loudness are associated with the most active effects of warm colours, the reverse true for the cool colours. It is understood that we as humans mentally connect a loud red with one that is of high saturation. This in most cases rare, when one speaks of a loud blue or green, the obvious being that high-pitched sounds tend to be grouped with the saturated light hues.

Therefore, the perception of noise and sound, may lead one to consider the perception of volume, frequently, found that lightness is one of the most important factors in our perception when it comes to open interior spaces.

Yet, light and neutral colours increase a room's size as would cool colours, it is therefore suggested that dark or saturated hues decrease a room's size as would warm colours.

It is then worth noting that a high illumination level will enlarge the appearance of volume, whilst a low illumination level will weaken it. Frieling (1980) below mentions just a few sound associations to various colours. As follows:

1. Red: Trumpet/loud

2. Pink: Soft/delicate, minor key

3. Gold-Yellow: Fanfare/major key

One factor that may be wise to consider when studying colour are the fundamentals of colour harmonies and combinations. As environments in today's world of work are always changing, the awareness of traditional colour harmonies are vital in understanding why various colour mix and some don't.

One particular analysis conducted by Mahnke (1996) describes the six colour harmonies. See below for the following:

1. Monochromatic: Where one hue varies in value and saturation e.g. pale green with dark green.

2. Analogues: A combination of no more than three colours e.g. blue, green-blue. Believed to offer more variety.

3. Complementary: Hues, which are directly opposite to one another.

4. Analogous-Complementary: Modification of the complementary scheme. Thus, harmony is achieved by choosing 2 colours that are next to each other.

5. Split-Complementary: Consists of one colour and the tones of two adjoining its complementary colour complements.

6. Double-Complementary: Recommends the use of two closely related hues and their complements.

So far, you have read the perception of noise, sound, volume and the fundamentals of colour harmonies. Now, you will have the prospect to grasp an insight of colour and its existence. Such factor that can be discussed here is the human vision. Our sense to see colour.

The human vision is regarded as one of the richest senses an individual possesses as it the sense that provides us, the human, with a wealth of information, and which we could not receive without light.

Figure 1.8 is an illustration of the human eye

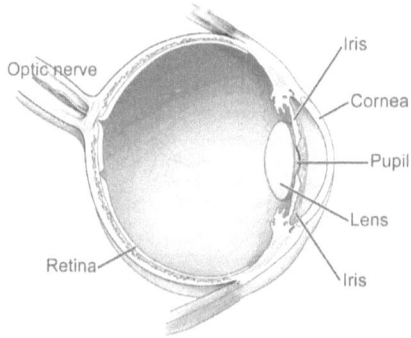

The human eye has both internal and external muscles; the internal muscles of the eye control the focus and the pupil. Whilst the external muscles of the eye point to an interest and work together to keep both eyes centred upon it.

Nonetheless, it is suggested that colour only exists in our brain and is the result of differentiating wavelengths of light that stimulates certain parts of our brain. According to neurophysiologists, colour is a strong stimulus, which we receive from the exterior world.

Evidently, colour is beyond neurophysiological associations, theory has it that colour healers believe in Chakras, energy centres that exist outside of our body, but within the aura. In scientific terms, the Chakras are in communication with the autonomic nervous system. As illustrated in Mahnke (1996), there are seven spectral colours. (As can be seen in figure 1.9.

Figure1.9 illustrates the Seven Chakras; a re-hybrid version of Mahnke's (1996) illustration

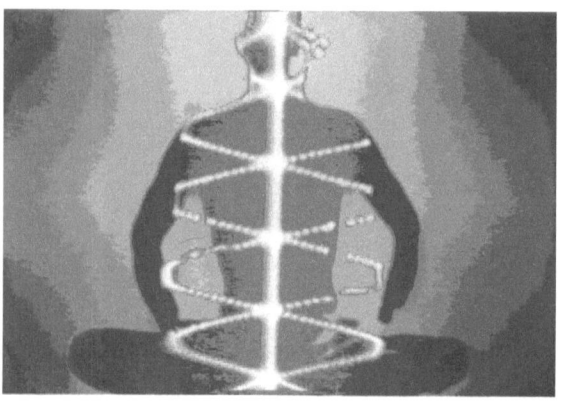

1. Vertex Chakra (Violet): Wisdom and spiritual energy.

2. Forehead Chakra (Indigo): Intuition.

3. Larynx Chakra (Blue): Creativity and religious inspirations, also communication.

4. Heart Chakra (Green/Pink): Love, influences the heart and thymus gland.

5. Solar Plexus Chakra (Yellow): Knowledge and intelligence.

6. Spleen Chakra (Orange): Energy influences the spleen and the pancreas.

7. Basis Chakra (Red): Life and reproduction, influences the sex glands and sexual organs.

Chakras explain an in-depth analysis that colour plays an imperative part of spiritual needs that an individual has. As such, for instance the colour red is assigned to the impatient, hot-tempered trail-blazing leader Aries. Given to Aries is the Planet of Mars, the God of War, which is symbolised by the colour red.

And, finally it all comes to an end with the first chapter describing the final alliance that may be considered as an association of colour. One such factor is psychosomatics; Felton (1994) described psychosomatics as Psycho-Neuro – Immunology (PNI) that is a close relationship which exists between the psyche and the physical well-being.

Colour devotes itself to the very grounds of neurophysiology, colour, and in fact is used to diagnose disorders such as colour blindness. Colours are widely used in the field of medicine; such tests used for patients with colour blindness, often involves a plate (a mixture of two or three colours); the patient than asked to detect the number merged in the colours; which means the observer will in effect have to discriminated between various hues.

So what about colour and brightness? Is there a link? Yes, it is pretty much so; colour can actually be arranged in accordance to the level of brightness. Human beings with normal colour vision can in effect distinguish over seven million different colour shades.

2

Feng Shui

Tradition and application for successful businesses

...What is life without meaning...man and his "things" (objects)...symbolism. The art of Feng Shui, yet not so common in west. One is fascinated and that indulges in our sub-conscious as a powerful tool. Without a second thought it has a meaning, a chair, a pen, or even a tea-cup. No rationality, it plays a symbolically part of our everyday life...

As humans we dismiss things that we don't understand, and remain ignorant...yet we are not satisfied if we don't label such elements. The teachings and applications of Feng Shui (also pronounced as Fung Soy or Fung Schway) are not so common in the west. Why?

Quite frankly, Feng Shui originates from China and the Orient; it dates back as early as 300BC when it was first developed in agriculture. The Chinese became aware of the Feng Shui teachings and used this as guidance as to where they grew their crops, placed their cattle, and even build their homes.

In fact, Feng Shui was the official secret and had only been practiced by the Emperor in the Imperial Palace and the Government. But, since then, has made its way through the wider world. The word Feng Shui means *Wind* and *Water*, which creates harmony and balance; historically regarded as the original elements of creation.

The words Wind and Water in its own right offer grounds for creativity. Take for instance a picture of a water fall can actually illustrate a meaning of soothing calmness to the soul, but to a person who is unhappy or juggling a jammed mind; may see it as noise and distraction. However, it is wise to note that the term Wind denotes intelligence.

Feng Shui consultant Stephen Buss graduated from Art College in 1974; worked under one of the world's foremost respectful experts, Master Joseph Yu at the Feng Shui Research Centre in Toronto. Buss developed an adaptation of the five elements according to the Chinese astrology associating colours and shapes.

Figure 2.1 illustrates the five elements associating colours and shapes, a chart developed by Buss

WATER	
Colour	Dark blue, grey or black
Shapes	Wavy or irregular
Example	Dark blue curtains, grey walls and ceilings
WOOD	
Colour	Green, blue green

Shapes	Long, thin, rod shaped
Example	Plants, trees and poles
FIRE	
Colour	Red, pink, orange and purple
Shapes	Triangular
Example	Red fire, candles, strong lights
EARTH	
Colour	Brown, yellow, Beige
Shapes	Square, rectangular
Example	Wooden tables, ceramic plant pots
METAL	
Colour	White, silver, gold
Shapes	Round, oval
Example	Metal and round objects

Another particularly interesting individual worth bearing in mind if you are thinking of creating successful businesses, and would like to know more about how Feng Shui applications could benefit you; can be seen in figure 2.2, which is a qualitative case study.

Figure 2.2
Case Study
Thomas Coxon Associates

Thomas Coxon graduated with Bachelor of Science, Master of Philosophy, and Fellow of the British Computer Society, Reiki Master and Feng Shui Master. His interests are primarily focused on the Earth's energy and Feng Shui. Coxon, Feng Shui Consultant, has been trained with some of the world's best Chinese and Tibetan Feng Shui Masters. As an empirical insight into what Coxon offers for individual's who may want to excel their business, or for personal development.

Coxon was asked several questions with regard to Feng Shui, the responses were collected qualitatively; an insight into how such application can improve the way we look at the energies we receive and project.

According to Coxon, his definition of science is that it has an underlying theoretical foundation with much more research, whereas an engineering discipline has a base of rules, when followed creates repeatable and predictable results. Thus, Feng Shui is more like engineering as it has both rules and calculations, if followed precisely, the results are both repeatable and predictable. Yet, what seems to be the missing piece of the jigsaw is the underlying base for theoretical research that has led to those rules being created. And, begs the question, as quoted by Coxon (2007) "then, from whence did the rules come? That is a question to which I have not yet found a satisfactory answer."

It has vaguely been understood that engineering plays some role in Feng Shui, and whether it is a science, is yet to be defined. The second question that often lurks in my sub-conscious- is can it be psychological, as often I wonder if it's just common sense. Well, according to psychologists, there is a thing called the "placebo effect," in which case things tend to turn out in the manner in which people expect them to. Coxon found that with his experience that surrounds around that it operates independently, though obviously harnessing the "placebo effect" to work alongside with Feng Shui rather than against it, which is generally sensible to do.

So far, it has been insightful into the realms of Feng Shui, but, and a huge but! Can Feng Shui with the application of colour work in organisations? Well, as it turns out; it can. Coxon, found that colour and Feng Shui, is often very much used by the press, probably because it is much easier to discuss and its elements of photography.

The reality for colours are that they are just one of the several ways of changing the influence, which a building and its surroundings have on us. Generally, individuals do get them about right, but there are some specific rules to follow in terms of working out how each group of colours interact, this is frequently associated with the five elements (wood, water, earth, fire and metal).

With regard to what has already being discussed; why study Feng Shui? I look at this question in more personality and astrologically based; for instance, individuals born under Sagittarius, Capricorn or even under the Scorpion, are very intuitive and sensing, which arouses many of us to travel deep to unknown realms, the excitement of mystery. Thus, one may study Feng Shui purely because it tells us how our surroundings influence us, how those influences can change over time, and what we can do to modify them, to some degree helps us master our own destiny. Feng Shui thus, plays a central role in our emotions; how? As a generalisation, if people are placed in surroundings which they find comfortable, they are likely to be much happier, as if their live was going well they would again enjoy a wealth of happiness.

A further generalisation, if buildings, which apply their colours and layouts; designed in ways which comply with the Feng Shui rule base, generally feel a lot nicer than those who haven't, so again the occupants tend to be happier. Yet, something that regularly popped in to my sub-conscious is what Coxon mention about astrology and Feng Shui, he states that there are specific influences based on an individual's birth date, which can be tweaked to directly influence their happiness. Similarly, there are influences which could be enhanced to create turmoil and conflict, usually one identifies that as those naturally present and tones them down, but the reverse could also be done.

To many, however, Feng Shui may not be so common, yet surprisingly Coxon reveals that many of his clients are: "Pop Stars, International Artists, Doctors, Lawyers, Accountants, Dentists, Architects, Builders, Management Consultants, Travel Agents, Recruitment Agencies, Property Investors, Racing Stables, Motor Racing Teams, Hotels, Restaurants, Schools, Super Markets, Post Offices, Garages, Manufacturers, Wholesalers, Distributors & Retailers of many kinds, major Computer Companies, Therapists, Hair Salons & Training Companies."

A mouthful to say the least, who would have thought that so many of us, from all walks of life, actually believe that by adapting Feng Shui in our lives can be rewarding and prosper success, the Chinese often call this the "Chi," which is another word for energy also called a "Life Force," but it differs in various countries, take for instance in India, they call it the Prana.

One general rule that is associated the Chi, is that the more you have it, the better; but may also be an over simplification. One could start by subdividing the Chi into Yin and Yang (negative polarity and positive polarity rather than "good and bad") into the five elements, (may consider these as the five flavours to the energy) which in turn can influence one's income, career, or even their health.

The Chi energy also leads to the connection between Feng Shui and astrology; and even better how this can prove to enhance successful businesses. Using astrology and Feng

Shui a business can truly succeed. For instance, a business has a start date and a horoscope though it's not calculated very often, and the Feng Shui of the buildings they're in, definitely influence the performance of the business.

An example of one type of business that used the applications of Feng Shui is HSBC, and in many cases is the most extreme example of that in recent times, but lesser examples are common. In simplest, HSBC employed the services of some of the top Feng Shui Masters around that time in the Far East (so the top guy in the world at the time) to work with their architect on the design of their new HQ in Hong Kong in the early 1980's.

Since then they've gone from "one of the pack" in terms of local regional banks to where they are now. Which is pretty much on every high street in the world. They have apparently, so to speak, have also moved their HQ to Singapore to get around a limitation of the Hong Kong site according to one of Coxon's source.

A quote for those who wish to prosper in success and happiness… *"Feng Shui, when properly applied, can only then make our mind, body and soul happy, enjoy life and achieve our goals…badly applied can only do the opposite…"*

Thomas Coxon (2007)

My understanding of Feng Shui is all about getting the "Chi" right. This is a Chinese concept that teaches one-that there is always constant energy flowing everywhere. The Chi energy symbolises life, health and prosperity. The Chi affects all our lives. The energy that I simply see as common sense. Take for instance; if a person is depressed or upset, he or she must pay attention to the Chi energy that flows within the house.

Feng Shui environmentalists believe that all individuals are connected to the Chi and the environment. The Chi energy is everywhere, around the earth and even around our body. The Chi is also regarded as Yin and Yang. Both Yin and Yang play a vital role in Feng Shui also known as the way of Heaven and Earth. Nothing in the world is without a balance. There can't be joy without sorrow.

Here is a little wisdom from Tom Coxon (2007), especially for those of you who are starting out SME's; according to Coxon, Feng Shui can be applied as most of his clients are in this category.

In theory the percentage benefit is likely to be more or less independent of size of company. However, the larger companies have bigger budgets so they can afford to pay their practitioners more.

This can help them in two ways: firstly they can afford, if they so desire, to hire pretty much any practitioner they chose. Secondly some practitioners vary the level of the Feng Shui they use depending on the fee - the more they're paid the more beneficial their advice. So overall the larger companies are likely to receive more beneficial advice, providing they are smart enough to recognise the top practitioners and pay them the going rate. (To give you a bench mark at the very top of the scale, the practitioner who advised HSBC back in the 1980's charged them £300 per square foot - at least £7 Million assuming that it was worked out on the land area, not per floor).

And Finally, Coxon was asked whether he had any tips on business success and personal development; and frankly it's worth bearing in mind... however, there aren't any easy ones - not that work well, or all the time anyway. Coxon's advice to those who want to get on (business and personal) is to take care of the Feng Shui along with the financial planning, the marketing, the production etc, etc.. In other words Feng Shui is just one aspect of a business that needs attention along with everything else. My second piece of advice, at least as far as the Feng Shui is concerned is to do their research about the practitioners who are out there, hire the one who will do the best job for the money they are willing to commit and implement their advice systematically and completely. Then monitor and learn from the results.

3

Astrology and I ...

I often get muddled with the term astrology; we tend to associate astrology with sun signs that you find in the last few pages of a magazine or a newspaper. The term astrology (best known as astronomy) according to the Oxford English Dictionary (1995), **astronomy** *n.* the study of stars and planets and their movements.

Historically, astronomy derives from the Arab and Persian astrology. In fact, the traditions and its application, astrology employs many concepts; its earliest recording dates back to the 2nd millennium BC that played a significant role in the shaping of culture. Astrology (*astronomy*) is a desire to be able to predict the future.

Many of its proponenets, astrology has been associated as being an art form, science, divination and symbolic. However, the scientific community labels astrology (*astronomy*) as pseudo (*fictional*) science. Astrology in some ways has been mocked in its teachings.

Much of astrology was used by the Muslim world around the 8th Century, while Europe was going through its Dark

Ages. Much of the astrological knowledge was driven by the classical sciences, mathematics, geography, astronomy and philosophy. Persian astronomer and astrologer Abu Rayhan Al Biruni *circa* 1000 made an early semantic distinction between astrology and astronomy.

According to the *Arabic* scriptures on astronomy it was studied by Caliph- Al-Mansur in Baghdad, who had also established the world's astronomical centre. Thus, knowledge was much increased by the Arabs.

Figure (?) illustrates a short list for some of the stars with its prominent and original names

STAR NAME		MEANING
Achemar	_____	Rivers End
Aladfar	_____	Claws
Aldebaran	_____	The Follower
Altair	_____	Sheep's tail
Betelgense	_____	The flying
Denah	_____	Central hand
Mitzar	_____	Waistband
Rasolgeth	_____	Head of the kneeling one
Rigel	_____	Foot of the Great one
Vega	_____	The falling

----O----

…Where would mankind be without his symbols, we look for meaning, and thus we place on a symbol with its own significance…

----O----

Astrology is all about symbols, in fact, astrologers use a chart to predict future events using illustrative symbols of the planets. Figure (?) diagram of the astrological glyphs for some of the planets *(also includes the Sun, the Earth, the Moon and Pluto).*

Figure (?) illustrates the astrological glyphs

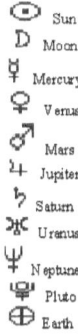

Surprisingly, however, the origins of astrological doctrines and methods developed later in Asia, Europe, and the Middle East among the Babylonians and their system of Celestial omens that began to comply around the 2nd Millennium BCE. But, it doesn't just stop there, Astrology is far wider than Man could imagine.

Colour in fact is associated to astrological signs and can tell a lot about a person. The astrological sign for a Scorpion is associated with the colour green/blue; such combination is connected to the thymus Chakra (See chapter one). The thymus Chakra portrays one expressing his or her heart felt emotions, however when confronted. The Scorpion has the ability to repress these feelings.

Both the green/blue combination therefore empowers the Scorpion to adapt to change and express their feelings with conviction without pleasing others. While the Sagittarian associates with the colour blue and is the sign for communication. The energy from the colour blue connects to dimensions of translating information; and thus the colour blue is related to the throat. While roaming around colours allied with shades of blue, indigo is often a mix of blues and greens. Such a sign that allies with the colour indigo, is the sign Capricorn, the sign is particularly mysterious as it possesses profound insights. An MBTI (Myers' Briggs Type Indicator) typology would then be Intuition (N). The colour indigo represents empathy and reinforcement.

Whereas a slightly more different colour aside from the blue/green/indigo, is the colour violet. The colour violet represents the sign Aquarius, also regarded as the crown Chakra- Mind. Individuals born under this sign are creative and inventive. The colour violet also plays a vital role for an MBTI typology of Thinking (T) and Perceiving (P). Violet, thus, is related to knowledge driven by a spiritual connection.

However, strong colours such as Magenta, finds its relationship with the sign Pisces. Both the sign and the colour are mentally effective and hold an MBTI typology of the Judging (J) characteristic. Individuals born under the sign Pisces are always on a mission to help others without wanting anything in return, the colour violet therefore offers vision. However, to say the least the Pisces also has the Aries fire, as it interconnects with the colour red.

The colour red is solely taken by the sign Aries, the Greek God of War, ruled by the planet Mars. Individuals born under this sign are trail blazers and pathfinders. They are great starters. But, they soon hand it over to someone else to finish. The Aries is a typical Extravert (E), an MBTI analysis of Act first, think and reflect later. The colour Red is loud and is connected to the sense for hearing combined with abundance of vitality. Red, in its own right is dynamic.

Both the colour and the sign Aries, are extremists physically, mentally and most assuredly emotional. An Aries associated with the colour red, is temperamental, never likes to be out done, and whose walk is almost like a run. A fantastic individual for positions that involve sales, to let this particular being open its marketing flare. However, an Aries is very id driven (Freud's psychoanalysis on id), and can often if not most of the time very demanding. Thus, the colour red offers the Aries energy for physical endurance.

While the Taurus links it self with the combination of red and orange. Individuals born under the sign Taurus are regarded as strong minded and able to overcome hurdles. Red is the energy for passion, and the colour orange is sensing which makes up the (S) typology for MBTI (Sensing).

Yet, individuals born under the sign Gemini exclusively only associate with the colour orange, this reflects that a Gemini is likely to think outside the box (creativity), however is often inconsistent and be too-demanding and childish, moments when they are like to be id driven, these individuals would work well as recruitment consultants where high income may be an incentive. Again, the colour orange is Sensing (S) and Feeling (F), reflecting a harmonious and creative aura.

In comparison, the sign Cancer also acquaints with the colour orange, but also yellow, thus the sign Cancer is also the first water sign in astrology. Individuals born under the sign Cancer are emotional and sensitive. However, they are more likely to be elf assertive. Individuals under the sign Cancer also combine with the colour blue; as like the Scorpio strive for mystery and psychological gratification.

Here, is where it gets a little exciting, the sign Libra is compatible to the art of Feng Shui; the balance between Yin and Yang. The Libra represents balance (e.g. the good and the bad). Individuals born under the Libra sign crave spontaneous but are also sensing and feeling 'beings.' Often the Libra is unemotional and airy. However, the colour green enables one to be less impatient.

The last to astrological signs that I would like to mention here is Virgo and Leo. The sign Virgo associates itself with the colour navy blue or grey. Thus, those who are born under the sign Virgo obsess for perfection which can often leave you dissatisfied. A Virgo strives for authoritarian figure; preferably a parent. The colours navy blue and grey empowers the Virgo to become more self motivated and letting go of control as well as overcoming this fear of not being accepted.

And, finally the sign Leo, surprisingly associates with the colour yellow. Unlike the Virgo, the Leo (and individuals born under this sign); doesn't feel the need to please others, however, this can be due to feeling undervalued by others. Thus, being popular is your goal. The colour yellow allows the Leo to express romance; creativity in themselves. Your challenge is to connect to and find value with your own core self; as Jung defines one of his archetypes as realising the self.

4

A Colourful Life

Dr. Nigel Marlow

"…Lead a colourful life"! That is an epitaph that some of us would like to have remain behind after our eventual final journey to either the lightness and whiteness of eternal Heaven or the foreboding darkness and blackness of infernal Hell. Yes! There are colours there as well! So we can lead a colourful death too! There is a clear difference in the colour palette on offer; light, white and golden or dark, black and crimson. Colour is all around us in our lives and we are led to believe that it will follow us into our immortality as well.

We all attach a great importance to colour. This can be a conscious attempt to study it closely as it appears in the natural world, adding to our delight of plants, flowers, trees and the exotic fauna of bird plumage or the simple puzzle of the piebald cow. An aesthetic pleasure is also derived from the inspection of the colour in paintings and other man-made pieces of art.

However, the subtlety of colour impinges on our senses at a sub-conscious or subliminal level as well. Colour surrounds our lives in an often under-appreciated manner. We are not always aware of the influence of colour in our everyday lives but it can affect the way we behave, the way we think and most importantly, how we feel.

This gives colour a remarkable and powerful involvement in shaping our everyday human experience. Colour affects our emotions; and it does so when we consciously inspect and evaluate it, or when we automatically 'like or dislike' something (or somebody)! It gives our worldly lives meaning, without colour life would be purely a dull leaf through pages of thoughts and concepts, cognitive in form, pale, colourless, and lacking in any emotional warmth[1].

How does colour achieve this pre-eminence in our lives? Why is it so important in giving our experience of the world meaningful? Where does its meaningfulness come from?

The answer to these questions is to be found in our psychology.

Colour psychology, in what should be described as mature consumer societies (formerly *Western Civilisation*), is a relatively new field of study and is viewed with suspicion

---

[1] What is an Emotion? William James (1884), First published in Mind, 9, 188-205.

by the majority of mainstream academic psychologists. The scepticism is fuelled by the practitioners of 'colour psychology', who claim there are a number of reactions to colour which seem to be noted in most persons. These reactions are deemed to be initially psychological, but because of the integrated nature of the bodily systems, these psychological reactions can in turn influence the physiology of the patient (be they human or animal).

Throughout history colour and light has been used by every culture, religion and society in a variety of ways in an attempt to treat disease. Colour Psychologists claim that by altering the colours which surround individuals, the person's state of health can be altered.

Colour therapists consider an individual's *aura*. This is considered to be an array of colours that emanates from all living beings. The colour therapist studies this aura either by concentration or behind a Kilner screen (two sheets of glass which have a cyanine dye encapsulated between them).

Colour therapists believe that each organ, body part, emotion or mental state responds to a specific colour. By observing the colours in an individual's aura the therapist can then use colour to treat those aspects that seem to be lacking in health.

This belief in the connection between colour and health has a long history. Ancient Egyptians used coloured minerals, stones, crystals, salves and dyes as remedies, and sanctuaries painted in various shades in treatment.

This interest in the physical nature of colour developed in Ancient Greece alongside the concept of the elements - air, fire, water and earth. These fundamental constituents of the universe were associated with the qualities of coolness, heat, wetness and dryness, and also the four humours or bodily fluids - choler or yellow bile, blood (red), phlegm (white) and black bile.

These bodily humours were thought to arise in four organs - the spleen, heart, liver and brain - and to determine emotional and physiological disposition of a person. Health involved the proper balance of these humours, and various diseases their mixture in wrong proportion. Colour was intrinsic to healing, which involved restoring the balance. Coloured garments, oils, ointments and salves were used to treat specific diseases.

In the near-East during the middle-Ages, the Persian physician Avicenna (980 - 1037) developed a treatise that expounded the vital importance of colour in both diagnosis and treatment. Following the Ancients, Avicenna noted that colour was an observable symptom of disease, and he developed a chart that related colour to temperament and the physiological condition of the body. He also advocated the use of colour in treatment, insisting that red moved the blood, blue or white cooled it, and yellow reduced pain and inflammation.

'Colour consultants' continue this arcane knowledge and practice today. They claim that hues in the red area of the spectrum are typically viewed as "warm" while those in the blue and green range are typically viewed as "cool".

Reds are also viewed as active and exciting, while the blues and greens are viewed as soothing and passive.

Black is considered as evil and malevolent and yet, on the other hand, it also stands for elitism and style.

White is associated with purity whereas grey is viewed as dull or boring.

In another system, red is considered to motivate action; orange and purple are related to spirituality; yellow cheers; green creates relaxation and warmth; blue relaxes; and white is associated with either purity or death.

It is probably true to say that there are as many meanings to the different hues in the electromagnetic spectrum as there are writers on the subject. As a 'rule-of-thumb' the table below summarises the meaning associated with colours (in Western cultures):

Colour	Associated Meaning
Gray	Elegance, humility, respect, reverence, stability, subtlety, wisdom, anachronism, boredom, decay, decrepitude, dullness, dust, pollution, urban sprawl, strong emotions, balance, neutrality, mourning, formality, March.
White	Reverence, purity, snow, peace, innocence, cleanliness, simplicity, security, humility, sterility, winter, coldness, criticism, surrender, cowardice, fearfulness, unimaginative, air, fire, death (Eastern cultures), hope, Aries, Pisces (star signs), bland, sterile, empty and unfriendly(interior), January.
Black	Modernity, power, sophistication, formality, elegance, wealth, mystery, style, evil, death (Western cultures), fear, anonymity, anger, sadness, remorse, mourning, unhappiness, mysterious, sex, seriousness, conventionality, rebellion, unity, sorrow, life, rebirth(ancient Egypt), slimming quality(fashion) January.
Red	Passion, strength, energy, fire, love, sex, excitement, speed, heat, arrogance, ambition, leadership, masculinity, power, danger, gaudiness, blood, war, anger, revolution, radicalism, socialism, communism, aggression, summer, autumn, stop, Mars (planet), respect, Aries (star sign), December. Studies show that red can have a physical effect, increasing the rate of respiration and raising blood pressure; red also is said to make people hungry; the red ruby is the traditional 40th wedding anniversary gift; red sky in the morning, shepherd's warning; red sky at night, shepherd's delight.

Blue	Seas, men, productive(interior) skies, peace, unity, harmony, tranquillity, calmness, coolness, confidence, conservatism, water, ice, loyalty, dependability, cleanliness, technology, winter, depression, coldness, idealism, obscenity, tackiness, air, wisdom, royalty, nobility, Earth (planet), Virgo (light blue), Pisces (pale blue) and Aquarius (dark blue) (star sign), strength, steadfastness, light, friendliness, July (sky blue), February (deep blue), peace, mourning (Iran), truthfulness, love, sadness, aloofness. In many diverse cultures blue is significant in religious beliefs, believed to keep the bad spirits away.
Green	Nature, bad spirits, spring, fertility, youth, environment, wealth, money (US), good luck, vigour, generosity, go, grass, aggression, inexperience, envy, misfortune, coldness, jealousy, disgrace (China), illness, greed, corruption (North Africa), life eternal, air, earth (classical element), sincerity, hope, Cancer (bright green, star sign), renewal, natural abundance, growth, health, August, balance, harmony, stability, calming, creative intelligence, Islam. During the Middle Ages, both green and yellow were used to symbolize the devil. Green is believed to be the luckiest of colours in some western countries including, Britain, Ireland (where it is also the national colour) and the U.S.
Yellow	Sunlight, joy, happiness, earth, optimism, intelligence, idealism, wealth (gold), summer, hope, air, liberalism, cowardice, illness (quarantine), hazards, dishonesty, avarice, weakness, greed, femininity, gladness, sociability, summer, friendship, Gemini, Taurus, Leo (golden yellow, star signs), April, September, deceit, hazard signs, death (Middle Ages), mourning (Egypt), courage (Japan). Yellow ribbons were worn during times of warfare as a sign of hope as women waited from their men to return. During the Middle Ages, both green and yellow were used to symbolize the devil.

Purple	Envy, Sensuality, bisexuality, spirituality, creativity, wealth, royalty, nobility, ceremony, mystery, wisdom, enlightenment, arrogance, flamboyance, gaudiness, mourning, profanity, exaggeration, confusion, homosexuality, pride, Scorpio (violet, star sign), May, November, riches, romanticism (light purple), delicacy (light purple). Purple is the colour of mourning for widows in Thailand, favourite colour of Egypt's Cleopatra, and the purple heart - given to soldiers who have been wounded during warfare.
Orange	Hinduism, Buddhism, energy, balance, heat, fire, enthusiasm, flamboyance, playfulness, aggression, arrogance, gaudiness, over-emotion, warning, danger, autumn, desire, Sagittarius (star sign), September. Orange has less intensity or aggression than red and is calmed by the cheerfulness of yellow. Orange is the Royal family of the Netherlands and symbolises royalty. The colour is associated with Protestantism in Northern Ireland.
Brown	Calm, depth, natural organisms, nature, richness, rustic, stability, tradition, anachronism, boorishness, dirt, dullness, filth, heaviness, poverty, roughness, earth (classical element), October, Capricorn, Scorpio (reddish brown, star signs), down-to-earth. Brown can stimulate the appetite, wholesomeness, steadfastness, simplicity, friendliness, and dependability.
Pink	Spring, gratitude, appreciation, admiration, sympathy, femininity, health, love, June, marriage, homosexuality.

As indicated, the meanings associated with the different colours are peculiar to Western cultures. The emphasis here should be on the words *culture* and *associated.*

When we examine the psychological effects of colour, it is important to understand that any effect on thinking, behaviour or feeling will be brought about because of the *meaning* that the colour has for the individual observer. Without a *meaning* the colour itself is psychologically neutral, it is an *empty-stimulus.*

How does colour come by this meaningfulness? The answer is that it doesn't! Colour itself has no meaning; its relevance to the individual depends on the cluster of associations that are *automatically* triggered in the observer's cortex by viewing that particular colour. These associations are <u>learned</u>. This learning takes place as an individual develops into adulthood through the processes of socialisation and enculturation. There may also have been some idiosyncratic contact with colours that an individual has experienced, so that particular hues will have episodic memories/associations for that person. Thus the meaning of a colour to an individual will thus depend upon previous experience of that colour in that person's life. The meaning of a colour will be generally accepted to the extent that everyone has had the same experience or learning (culture) about that colour, but individuals in addition may have peculiar nuances of meaning associated with that hue. We would also expect that colours have different meanings in different cultures.

Those of you who have studied semiotics will now recognise that colour is a particular sign, and what it signifies depends on the observer's knowledge (both consciously accessible and implicit). Colour is what Charles Peirce[2] would classify as a *symbolic* sign.

Thus the answer to the question, "What meaning is conveyed by colours that surround us in everyday life?" is "It depends!" It depends on the culture and to some extent the individual. The question is further complicated by the fact that colours seldom occur singly in the environment. Colours usually occur in different combinations. How do the different combinations change the meaning of individual colours? And what overall meaning do the different combinations convey?

The commercialisation of our society and 'consumerisation' of our culture means that we are all becoming increasingly sensitive to use of colour. Colour surrounds us whether it is from nature, buildings or increasingly from the scenery of the 'shopping theatres' in our high streets. The new cathedrals of consumption, the super-hyper markets and the stores contain kaleidoscopes of colour within their product displays, advertising, and stylish pyramids of

[2] Peirce, C. (1934). *Collected papers: Volume V. Pragmatism and pragmaticism.* Cambridge, MA, USA: Harvard University Press.

packaging. It is from this area of commerce where the main pressure to grasp the real meaning of colour arises; the marketers and advertisers wish to use colour more effectively.

Any study of this area needs first to examine the different levels of meaning conveyed by particular colours. We have already identified two levels; those of cultural and individual. But there exists also a third level of meaning that has developed from the similar *universal* experience of colour by humans.

At this level colours prompt similar thoughts and emotions from almost everyone. For example red is the colour of flames in the fire and blood from a wound. We can all associate or empathise with the emotions of sitting around a warming fire, or a building burning or getting scorched by a lighted match. Blue is the colour of cooling waters, relaxation, and cleanliness and of the summer sky, signalling comfort, calmness and perhaps pleasant daydreaming. Green is the colour of vegetation and signifies associations with nature, growth, fruitfulness, freshness and ecology.

At a cultural level however, green can mean variously, good luck, seasickness or money. Blue on the other hand can represent sadness ("I have the blues") as well as the sky. And the energetic and aggressive red hue can also mean 'Halt'.

Thus in order to fully understand colours we need to bear in mind these different levels of meaning. In addition, we need to explore the meanings created by using different colour combinations and the interrelationship between colours.

For our complete dictionary of colour meaning we need also to be aware of the further consideration of how tonal changes of the same hue may have an affect. And finally, we need to address the question as to whether the saturation of a hue has any influence on the perceived meaning.

From our discussion above, we can see that an understanding of the world of colour is not easily achieved. However, because of the increasing importance of colour in our environments, such an understanding is worth working towards.

5

A Colourful Personality?

Dr. Nigel Marlow

Is there a connection between colour and your psychology? Does your preference for different colours reflect your personality somehow? Is your choice of favourite colours part of your personal characteristics and unchanging or does your likes and dislikes change with the mood that you are in?

According to Max Luscher there is a direct connection between your psychological make-up and your preference for certain colours. Luscher believed that each person's brain responds differently to colour and therefore different personality types prefer different colours.

He developed a simple colour test in 1947 that linked a person's choice of colours to both physical and mental states. The colour test is based on this and describes an individual's personality according to which colours are chosen and in what order. It has since been used and developed by doctors, psychiatrists, psychologists and recruitment personnel as an important tool in understanding the hidden aspects of personality.

The test itself is quite easy to complete and the instructions are straightforward[3]. A selection of cards of different colours are presented (either manually or on screen), and the individual makes a choice in order of preference.

The order of presentation is re-arranged and the procedure repeated.

The results are then analysed and interpreted using five dimensions that reflect different aspects of an individual's personality or self-concept.

The dimensions are:

1). Motivations or desired objectives.

2). Existing situation.

3). Characteristics held under conscious restraint.

4). Repressed characteristics.

5). Actual problems in reality.

The interpretation is based on a person's psychological condition at the time of test. The results can be affected

---

[3] The Luscher Colour Test by Ian Scott reviewed by John W. Conner in *The English Journal*, Vol. 61, No. 2 (Feb., 1972), pp. 302-303.

by current mood state, which is susceptible to the hassles and vagaries of daily life.

The Luscher analysis is based on these global meanings of colour. (This is not the full range of interpretations. The nuances of preference for colours when in combinations are detailed in Luscher's book).

RED: represents passion and energy. Red in the first position means the individual is impulsive, sexy and has a will to win. These people make good leaders. They want to expand their horizons and live a life to the full. Red in the seventh or eighth position means that desire for life and thirst for adventure has become diminished.

YELLOW: represents happiness and relaxation. Choosing yellow in second, third or fourth place is positive; it indicates an optimistic person who always looks to the future - never backwards. They find life easy, and problems simply do not exist for you. Free from worry, they lead a carefree life; but this does not mean that they are lazy. Yellow-choosers can be extremely hard-working, although not consistently so. Yellow chosen in first place means that the individual is ambitious and eager to please. When yellow is in the later part of the choice-spectrum, it indicates that they feel that their hopes and dreams have been dashed and they feel isolated and disappointed. This is often accompanied by behaviour that is defensive and withdrawn.

GREEN: indicates a doggedness and resistance to change. When chosen in first place the individual has persistent, possessive and maybe quite selfish characteristics. They are a high achievers and accumulators of possessions to reflect status and social standing. These people have a strong fear of failure and want to be recognised and have a powerful need to impress others. If green is a later choice, the ego has been bruised there is a sense of resignation to the obstacles being encountered in life's pathways. Subsequently such individuals can be highly critical, sarcastic and stubborn.

A mixture of red and blue, PURPLE represents a conflict between impulsiveness and calm sensitivity, dominance and submissiveness. The person who prefers violet wants to find a mystical, magical relationship. These individuals can be seen as romantics stuck in a dream-world of wishful thinking and fantasy. When violet appears in the later part of the preference sequence, it indicates that the person is mature and has outgrown the 'fantasy' vision of life preferring to confront life's harsh reality head-on.

BROWN: is the colour of perceived health and physical well-being. If low in the order of preference it indicates that the person is not very concerned about their health. and body. It probably means they are in good shape. Those worried about illness tend to put brown earlier in the sequence. Brown chosen as a favourite colour can indicate feelings of insecurity and restlessness.

GREY is a neutral hue and represents a point between two contrasting and motivations. Grey in the first position demonstrates a wish to shut the world out and remain uncommitted. Grey people dislike 'team-work' and being part of a group. They tend to be 'on the outside, looking-in' and are observers rather than a doers. When chosen lower in the preference ranking Grey suggests that the person is generally eager and enthusiastic about life. Such people have a high self-motivation and continually strive to achieve their goals.

BLUE represents calmness and loyalty. A person who favours blue is sensitive and easily hurt. They rarely panic and are in total control of life and content with the way it is going. Such people desire to lead an uncomplicated and worry-free life and are prepared to sacrifice certain goals in order to achieve this. They need a stable relationship without conflict. The later blue appears in the rankings, the more unsatisfied the person is. Such individuals have a sense of being 'trapped' and feel a tension in their daily lives from what they consider unnecessary restrictions (usually psychological) are and the more you feel the need to break from the ties that restrict you.

Choosing BLACK as a favourite colour is exceptional. It indicates a revolt against fate. Such individuals are prepared to give up everything in order to achieve their desires. In the lower ranking BLACK represents a feeling of control over one's life and a balanced outlook.

Psychologists who have gained training and experience using the Luscher Colour Test can be quite sophisticated with their diagnoses and interpretations of an individual's personality. As with anything this colour test can be misused and it is easy to see that poor interpretations or insensitive feedback to the client can be psychologically harmful. Of course, the Luscher test has been commercially published and unlike most robust psychometric personality tests is widely available to the public who have no professional training in the area of person-testing. So if you purchase a copy from your local bookstore or Amazon or ABE Books, please be careful, whether using the test on yourself and especially if you intend analysing others' personalities.

Apart from the original printed version, the WWW has spawned several websites that you can visit and complete a Luscher colour test on-line. Some of these test-sites are free to use because your participation is supporting an on-going research project. For a taste of what the Luscher test feels like, try the on-line test at this address: http://www.psycorr.com/Psich/fizE.htm. It is only a part of the full Luscher test and takes about two minutes to complete. Because of this, if you have a go, please treat the experience as a little fun or an initial 'dipping-the-toe-in'. The feedback is almost instantaneous in the form of an overview of your character.

Here is a summary of the feedback from my test:

> "Strong need of peace and relaxation; fatigue easily provoked by strains and stresses, striving for comfort, protection and peace.
>
> Wish to forget the past.
>
> Unsatisfied need of relaxation can provoke a depressive state.
>
> Strong need for calm, peace and harmony; need to protect self from irritation and agitation.
>
> Seeks a sense of community and harmony in contacts with other people.

Restricted and restrained excitement, which is provoked by the attempt to resist any pressure at all costs, leads to irritation, fits of anger, sexually neurotic states and complaints of love nature.

You consider the existing situation to be threatening and dangerous. You are indignant, because of the thought that you will be unable to achieve your aims and you are suffering a feeling of inability to change it. You feel indignation and irritation, because the successful execution of your plans can fail.

Has a developed fear of becoming dependent and/or lonely."

As you can see some of the feedback is quite negative and that is why I advise caution when using these tests unsupervised, even when only 'for fun'. How accurate is it? That would be telling! And be aware that there is a

---

[4] 'The Barnum effect' after P. T. Barnum's observation that 'we've got something for everyone' is the observation that individuals will give high accuracy ratings to descriptions of their personality that supposedly are tailored specifically for them, but are in fact vague and general enough to apply to a wide range of people. This is also known as the Forer effect, which can provide a partial explanation for the widespread acceptance of some of the pseudo-sciences such as astrology and fortune telling, as well as many types of personality tests. Barnum's other famous quote is "There's a sucker born every minute"!

certain 'Barnum Effect'[4] that may inflate the perception of the accuracy of the interpretation.

Could there be some other evidence for this proposed link between colour and personality? A series of intriguing studies has been conducted by Shigenobu Kobayashi during the 1960's into people's colour and design preferences. He has published over 30 books on colour but few of these have been translated from the original Japanese. There are three of his works available in English and are worth seeking out[5].

Kobayashi's work is interesting because he attempts to associate colours with what he calls 'image' words. The lists of 'image' words contain 180 items that range from evaluative adjectives e.g. delicate, through to moods and emotional state descriptors e.g. peaceful.

The image words are arranged in a matrix that is formed by two orthogonal axes. The vertical axis is a vector of 'material quality' and ranges from 'hard' to 'soft'. The horizontal axis indicates the 'level of excitement' contained in the material, and this dimension is anchored using 'warm' and 'cool' descriptors. The image words can thus be positioned within the matrix according to the level of their 'warmth' and degree of 'hardness'. Kobayashi has additionally nominated certain image words as being typical or 'representative' of certain bounded areas of the

---

[5] Published by Kodansha International Ltd., Tokyo.

matrix. These 'named' territories contain groups of image words that have a degree of overlap in their semantic or emotional meaning. They can be associated with one another without being considered synonyms. Below is a an adaptation of Kobayashi's matrix showing the two axes and some of the 'named territories';

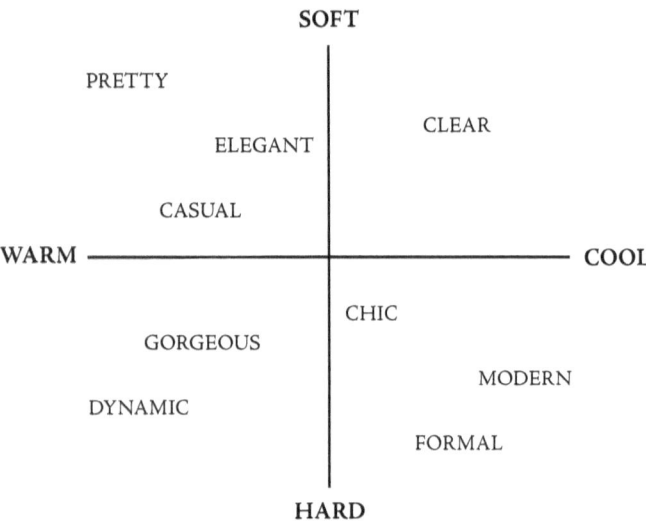

From his many studies, Kobayashi has also been able to construct a similar matrix for colours. Thus his 'Colour Image Scale' places for example, Pinks and Reds in the Warm and Soft quadrant, Pale Greens and Pale Blues in the Cool and Soft quadrant, Mauves and Olives fall in the Warm/Hard quadrant and Deep Browns and Deep Greens inhabit the Cool/Hard quadrant.

This method of describing and categorising colour and 'image words' as used by Kobayashi (1998) pays tribute to the methodology as used by Russell to analyse and categorise human emotions. Even a cursory inspection of the 'Colour Image Scale' and Russell's 'Circumplex Model' of emotion (see below) reveals obvious conceptual similarities.

Russell's Circumplex Model of Emotion[6]

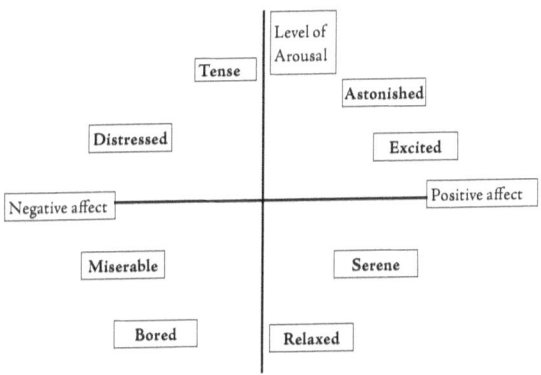

Russell's model (above) graphically illustrates his theory that <u>all</u> human affective states arise from two fundamental neurophysiological systems. One system is related to valence; a pleasure/displeasure evaluative dimension and the other is a dimension relating to the level of arousal or alertness.

Every human emotion can therefore be understood as some sort of combination or ratio of these two dimensions.

[6] Russell, J.A. (1980). A Circumplex Model of Affect. Journal of Personality and Social Psychology: 39, 1161–1178.

'Excited', for example, would be conceptualized as an emotional state that is the product of strong activation in the neural systems associated with positive valence together with moderate activation in the neural systems associated with arousal[7]. Affective states other than excitement likewise arise from the same two neurophysiological systems but differing in the degree or extent of activation. Specific emotions therefore arise out of patterns of activation within these two neurophysiological systems, together with cognitive interpretations and labelling of these core physiological experiences.

If we merge Kobayashi's terminology with that of Russell we get a model that looks like this:

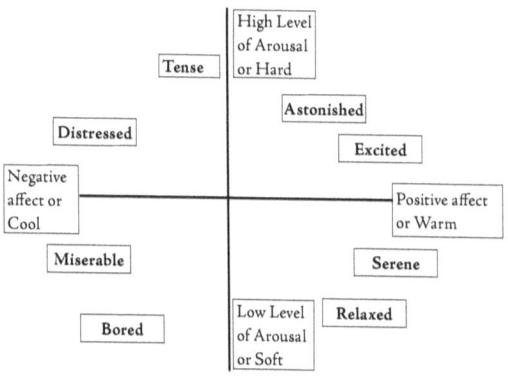

---

[7] These neural systems (not identified by Russell) may correspond to the sub-systems of the peripheral nervous system, the sympathetic and parasympathetic networks.

And if we add in some of the colours from Kobayashi's palette, the final model links colour, the characteristics of colour images, and human emotion thus:

The ReenMar© (RM) 'Colour of Emotion Model'

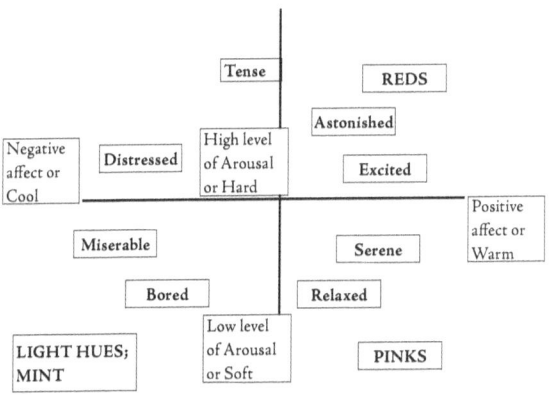

If we accept Russell's contention that emotions have a neurophysiological basis, and Kobayashi's taxonomy of colour images, we have an established link between colour and emotion. In other words the feeling, imagery or 'atmosphere' that colours produce in observers is based on the emotional reaction that they generate, and this in turn is a product of subtle and often fleeting transitions in the nervous system. Thus the *meaning* of colours is not entirely a product of socialisation and enculturation, but is at least partially individually determined by responses in the nervous system.

We can also find support for the relationship between colour and personality. In mainstream scientific Psychology there is a cadre of researchers and theorists who believe that personality is biologically determined. This paradigm, often known as the 'Trait' approach to personality, focuses on causal biological explanations of "The Big3"[8], which emphasize the relationships of biological mechanisms of emotional reactivity with dimensions of stable individual differences. These causal theorists contend that explanations of individual differences in personality can best be solved in terms of underlying neural mechanisms.

Individual differences in the functioning of these systems are believed to cause differential sensitivities to environmental cues (in our argument, this is colour and colour combinations), leading to differential affective and cognitive states. An individual's personality (a combination of the "Big3" Traits) is therefore defined according to the probabilities of having a specific reaction to certain environmental stimuli (colour).

We now have a link between the Eysenck's (and others e.g. Cloninger, 1987; Gray, 1994) work on the biological substrates of personality involving the traits of 'introversion-extraversion', 'neuroticism-stability', and 'socialization-psychoticism' and Luscher's analysis of personality based on individual colour preferences. Both have a basis in

---

[8] See the voluminous work of Hans Eysenck (e.g. 1967; 1990; 1991) on Extraversion, Neuroticism and Psychoticism.

delicate and yet profound sub-conscious reflexes in the nervous system.

These reflexes are generally subtle emotional responses based upon the fundamental (integrated biological and psychological) dimensions of *'approach- reward',' inhibition- punishment',* and *'aggression- flight.*

These three interrelated biological and behavioural systems are the sources of individual differences in emotional reactions to both environmental and internal stimuli (memories).

Our lives are indeed coloured by emotions and our emotions lived through colour!

References:

Cloninger, CR. (1987). A systematic method for clinical description and classification of personality variants - a proposal. Arch. Gen. Psychiatry, 44, 573-88.

Eysenck, HJ. (1991). Dimensions of personality: 16: 5 or 3? Criteria for a taxonomic paradigm. Personality and Individual Differences, 12, 773-90.

Gray, JA. (1994). Framework for a taxonomy of psychiatric disorder. In SHM van Goozen, NE van de Poll, & J Sergeant (Eds.), Emotions: Essays on emotion theory (pp. 29-59). Hillsdale, N. J.: Erlbaum.

6

Freud

Psychoanalysis and Colour

"The child is father of Man."
-William Wardsworth-

Freud believed that the mind was mind up of three levels: the conscious; sub-conscious; and the unconscious. Freud made a further association to the three levels of the human mind; he labelled these components as the id; ego; and the superego.

The first component according to Freud is the id also known as the "It." The id is completely irrational and emotional, and without a doubt is allied by the sub-conscious (unknown desires); it is driven by the libido, which is the pleasure principle, as the id constantly strives for gratification. Thus, the id is "I want it all…now."

The second component is the ego, which associates with "I." The ego is our rationality. The ego is the consciousness, frequently cold, boring and distant. The ego is aware of "we don't always get what we desire." And, that our consequences can "hurt me and others."

Finally the last part to in human development of the mind is our superego. The term used often is "Over Me" and is forever always guilty. The superego is our conscience

Freud described the id as irrational and emotional. To one, this denotes characteristics of an extravert, simply as they are outspoken, strive for constant satisfaction. To me, in particular this sounds like an individual that would suit best in roles of sales and recruitment, television and generally those who have a flare of creativity. Such individuals would be likely to be born under the signs; Aries, Pisces and Cancers.

Psychoanalysis in effect can work wonders for personal development and development. And your colour says it all (see Chapter 2 on astrological signs and colours).

Classical Psychoanalysis
versus
Colour Psychology

When studying classical psychoanalysis, the one theory that sticks to my mind is Freud (the founding father of psychoanalysis). So, this brings me to the next question; how can one possibly associate colour with Freud? Well, pretty easily. Have you ever wondered why it is that sometimes things just slip out, when quite rationally that is not what we intend to project.

According to Freud, it's our conscious ruled by the unconscious; this is also known as the Freudian slip, often believed to be our unconscious thoughts and feelings. One example: Jo is talking to Simon about how her mind is all over the place; rationally to come across as being overworked, accidentally says her mind is "erotic".

However, a psychoanalyst might tell you that this is much more than a random accident. The psychoanalytical view holds that there are inner forces outside of your awareness that are directing your behaviour. For example, a psychoanalytic theorist might say that Jo misspoke due to unresolved feelings that are somewhat repressed sexually.

7

Carl Jung

…One could ask what Jung could possibly contribute to the success of businesses, or even colour for that matter…if like me…you would know that anything is possible. Truth is businesses are now investing millions of pounds on consultants' world wide to increase profits, so, wouldn't it be great if one was to psychoanalyse businesses…

Two great minds are that of Jung and Freud (as mentioned in previous chapters); Jung's theory like Freud divides the human psyche into three parts. The ego, according to Jung is closely connected to the human conscious mind, which also allies itself with the collective unconscious, basically anything that is not conscious.

In other words, our unconscious mind holds all memories, even those that are repressed, and can often be brought up. Yet, one thing that makes Jung more vividly outstanding than any other theories (I almost find myself indulging in his world), is his concept of the collective unconscious (as mentioned in Chapter 1). Thus, the collective unconscious is referred as our "psychic inheritance."

The contents of the collective unconscious are labelled as the archetypes (worth noting for those who strive business success). Other names have been used alongside the label-"archetypes," such are dominants, imagos, mythological; but, most commonly referred to as archetypes.

The archetypes that Jung portrays of the collective unconscious are: the Mother; the Mana; the Shadow; the Persona; and finally the Anima and Animus. Such archetypes can actually be described using colours and is credible for interiors in general/or/office interiors such as, colours that are rich in flavour often being strong forceful colours like red, black, magenta can associate itself with the Persona.

So what exactly are archetypes? Well, the first archetype according to Jung is the Mother- this symbolises Earth (Nurturing). If an individual's mother failed to satisfy this need, the need to be loved, (Bowbly's attachment theory worth noting here), the person is likely to seek comfort throughout life. Therefore, colours such as soft blues and pinks are most likely to offer a pleasant atmosphere. And the very saying "life at sea" denotes the colour ocean blue.

The second archetype is the Mana-, which is not in any way associated with the so-called biological "things." The Mana seeks spiritual demands, for instance if one dreamt about the penis, Freud's interpretation would be that there is repressed unfulfilled need for sex, whereas Jung completely differs from that view, dreaming about sex is in no way associated with the phallus or that the person is in dire need for unfulfilled eroticism. In fact, in primitive societies, phallic symbols do not refer to sex.

The third archetype is the Shadow; in other words refers to sex and life instincts. The Shadow is our dark side of the ego, and the evil that we are fully capable of committing places itself there. The Shadow therefore is unethical and is neither good nor bad (Yin and Yang).

The fourth archetype is the Persona as mentioned vaguely earlier in this chapter. The Persona is the image we mask on ourselves before entering the outside world. The Persona falls as a distant part of our collective unconscious. We often associate colours such as black to be smart, elegant and generally sharp in appearance. Red, for instance, reflects an extraverted image, even if one is an introverted thinker (something to bear in mind).

Colours play a very important part to the Persona, we may associate colours such as pinks, sky blues, grass greens, to associate with hippies, socialists etc, quite frankly it all falls under the Johari's Window Theory, our impressions of others.

And, finally the fifth archetypes are the Anima and the Animus. Our gender and the role we play. Once again colours play a significant role, pink is most commonly associated with girls and the colour blue is associated with boys. Jung's definition of the Anima is the female aspect that is present in the collective unconscious of men; and the animus is the male aspect that is present in the collective unconscious of women.

According to both Freud and Jung, we are all really bisexual creatures in nature, from the very beginning; when we are foetuses, we have apparently undifferentiated sex organs until it comes under the gradual influence of hormones as to whether we become male or female.

Jung further mentions other archetypes that play a significant role in the society we live in. Such archetypes are the Child,- this portrays the Christ Child, that represents the future, rebirth, and deliverance; whilst the other archetypes involve the Father,- which depicts guidance and authority, hugely associated with dark colours such as black, navy blue and often red.

Can Jung's theory be relevant to personal development? Well, yes actually...Jung essentially describes a precise purpose in our existence that is distinctive in words, - such is, realising the "Self." The Self is also regarded as an archetype; the sole objective is when an individual is able to realise its self. They are in effect less selfish.

None the less, *Synchronicity* makes Jung's theory without a doubt one of the rare distinguished ones, that is not only comparable to parapsychology but tries to explain them. Synchronicity therefore is the occurrence of two events that are not link causally or connected teleologically; but are meaningful.

Jung, moving aside from the archetypes developed personality typologies that differentiated between extraversion and introversion. Throughout the chapters there are typologies that are mentioned. Jung's theory can enable an individual to progress their personal development. A huge number of businesses are wise to invest in this particular theory as it offers ground for contemporary research such as life; business and even personal coaches use such elements with regard to such models such as the STAR, GROW AND WHEEL OF LIFE.

8

Consuming nothing to consume everything: can Business Psychology help?

Dr. Nigel Marlow

Since the turn of the twentieth century, 'consuming' has gradually become more and more central to our way of life. Consuming is no longer just a matter of surviving. It has now become a 'lifestyle'. We define ourselves by our consumption patterns. What, where and when we buy says more about who we are than any CV. It tells others what tastes, values, interests and attitudes that we have. We readily display style and class through consuming 'things' and can even let others know about our fantasies and sexuality through the contents of our shopping trolley.

Traditional mechanisms that established social and status distinctions have been supplanted by acts of conspicuous consumption. It is the experiences of shopping and consuming 'things' have come to define our lives and our place in the social world. The costumes and props of our social roles are eagerly displayed by all kinds of actors who are identifying themselves and indicating social position and prestige through 'product clusters'.

Consuming has become a moral doctrine, a way of life. The 'good life' *is* the pleasure and enjoyment obtained through purchasing and using things. And *consumer choice* has now come to represent *the* desirable economic and political system. It is consumer demand that is *freeing* the old Soviet bloc and China. It is consumer choice that is championing democracy, self-determination and even freedom itself.

However, our consumer-led lifestyles are also leading us blindly along the path to self-destruction. We inhabit two worlds. 'Our' world is constructed through our complex relationships with symbols, symbols that speak god-like to our bicameral minds from the showroom, shop-window and TV screen. There is no reality except that we construct for ourselves. A Sartrian reality in which we can become what we seem to be. We live inside carefully constructed shells of identity that parade peacock-like in a temporary display of 'me' on the stage of infinity.

The other world is 'under the greatest threat' (Margaret Beckett, Environment Secretary, November 2005).

In this parallel world, global temperature increases will lead to the poorest countries facing a rising death toll from disease and malnutrition. Across this other planet, the paradox of rising sea levels[9] and water shortages will force the migration of whole populations with the associated geo-political conflicts. Who will open their borders for half of the population from Bangladesh?

Changes in the climate will also affect the richer nations too. There will be more frequent exceptional 'weather-events' such as those tearing through the Southern United Sates this summer[10] and even more alarming than a pandemic of bird flu is the possibility of equatorial insects reaching Europe carrying diseases such as malaria, Lyme disease and encephalitis.

We have only just woken up to the events in the 'other' world. In particular, 2005 has seen wide coverage of environmental issues and indications that climate change and global warming have finally been accepted as scientific fact. Responses at the Government level have ranged from re-supporting the Kyoto protocol promising to cut

[9] 'Sea level rise doubles in 150 years', Ian Sample, Independent, November 2005.
[10] Climate change can be likened in its destructive scale to the effects of using weapons of mass destruction, according to Lord May of Oxford. The devastation caused by Hurricane Katrina is an example of the sort of extreme weather event that climate change can trigger. (November 2005).

greenhouse pollution[11], to re-opening the discussion on the future use of nuclear power promising clean energy generation[12].

Even those advocating the development of alternative, non-carbon based sources of energy generation are missing the point. It is not a question of whether wind or wave! It is a question of how to reduce the need to produce unsustainable levels of energy. We must cut back: and especially in the consumer-led economies such as the UK and USA. A recent report (November, 2005) from the European Environment Agency showed that on average, an individual in the UK is currently devouring the planet's natural resources at a rate five times and a citizen of the USA nine times that of an inhabitant of Continental Africa.

The problem of global warming, climate change and environmental destruction is not one of how we produce energy but one of *how much*. It is not a problem of energy production but of energy consumption. We produce to

---

[11] Despite the fanfare, the Kyoto agreement is a fudge. One of its central tenets, The Clean Development Mechanism (CDM), relies on a system of 'Carbon Credits' whereby high-polluters can buy 'certified', transferable and bankable' Kyoto credits from low-polluters. The net effect of this is a negligible reduction in carbon emissions and a new, highly lucrative commodity market, the European end of which is known as the Emissions Trading Scheme (EU ETS).

[12] See this website for an example of the heritage of 'clean energy': http://www.angelfire.com/extreme4/kiddofspeed/chapter47.html

consume and over the last fifty years our consumption has increased until it is at an unsustainable level. Ironically, our oil supplies have reached 'peak production'[13] just as the economies of China and India are beginning to exercise their newly found freedom of 'consumer choice'. No amount of windmills or solar panels will be able to satiate this developing appetite for energy that is needed to produce all our 'essential' consumables.

This linkage between production and consumption is as old as humanity itself. Tool-making, farming and other technological developments have allowed us to produce what we needed to survive and even some surplus, which eventually gave rise to trading and the development of economies. However, in the time-span of Man's existence, it is only very recently that, like the climate, this relationship between production and consumption has become overheated.

It was the harnessing of machine power and systems theory that enabled Ford to astonish the business world at the turn of the twentieth century with 'assembly lines'. The first automated car plants were soon producing hundreds and then thousands of cars each week whereas before only a few handcrafted models left the factory gates. It was the dawn of mass production. It spread from car manufacturing to household goods and eventually to all consumer goods. Ford had given the world a way of producing things cheaply and lots of them!

---

[13] http://www.lifeaftertheoilcrash.net/

Initially, cheapness sold! Products such as cars that had been luxury items for the very rich suddenly became affordable to the bricklayer, baker and factory worker! Business and production boomed along with consumption levels and general living standards, measured in consumer goods, rose year upon year. The link between mass production and mass consumption was formed.

However, what was to happen as the hunger of the new mass consumer market became satiated? How could the manufacturers maintain the demand for the products of their Golem-like factories? When a family owned one black model-T Ford, would they want another, at any price? Looking at the problem rationally, not until the original had worn-out! It seemed obvious that only a certain number of products could be sold into a given market before capacity naturally settled purely to a replacement level. It seemed that 'Fordism' had its limits.

However, at this juncture Ford is joined by that other influential giant of the twentieth Century, Sigmund Freud! It wasn't Freud himself who made the compact with the production-men; the relationship between Fordism and Freudism was initially forged by his second cousin Edward Bernays. Spookily, Bernays had spent WW11 in developing propaganda for the USA War Department and with the cessation of hostilities, set about applying the same Freudian principles involved in mass psychology to the burgeoning consumer markets. His clients for 'motivational marketing' included General Electric, Dodge Motors, Proctor and Gamble and American Tobacco.

For the latter, in order to encourage women to take up smoking, cigarettes became 'Torches of Freedom'. It was the first time in history that products were being subtly marketed as 'something else' to consumers and rising sales showed that they loved it! Despite early warnings[14] the virus of this subconscious persuasion took hold and irrevocably warped consumption patterns wherever populations became convinced that the consumption of 'something else' would lead to the 'good life'.

What is this warping mechanism? For the answer we have to look at our psychology and the interplay between our subconscious, motivations and values. As human beings we come into this world with a bundle of needs that have to be satisfied for us to survive and thrive. Some of these needs are physiological such as the need for food, drink, sleep and sex.

But of equal importance are our psychological needs, which are part a blessing and part a burden associated with the development of our intricate brains. Examples of our psychological needs are the need for friendship, the need to love and be loved, the need 'to be somebody', and, perhaps the most nagging, the need to find a meaning in life. It is

---

[14] The seminal work is 'The Hidden Persuaders' by Vance Packard, 1953.

this set of psychological needs that separates humans from the rest of the animal kingdom. And *all* humans are born with this *same* collection of requirements that have to be satisfied for a healthy existence.

YES! All humans have the same set of needs whether they live in the North, South, East or West! The reason that great differences occur is that we *learn* to *value* different things to satisfy those *same* needs. Just consider the need for food to satisfy hunger. A visit to the local supermarket will demonstrate the variety of food items that are each *valued* differently by some customer over another. Will it be mince, spam, or sausage tonight; perhaps snails or frogs legs; horse flesh? Sorry, you might be vegetarian, and have a completely different set of *values*.

This range of eating behaviour is mirrored with the variety of behaviours that are valued to satisfy the needs for drinking, sleeping, safety and sex. This diversity in values becomes a mind-boggling assortment when we think about 'other' genders, age-groups and cultures.

But in the consumer-led economies there is an additional complexity added to the mixture. It is not just a choice between the perceived values of product categories; we also have a choice between *brands*. So it is not just a decision concerning a tin of beans or peas, it becomes a pick from Heinz or Bachelors or Tesco's own brand. If we were rational, the choice is trivial because *any* brand would satisfy the need for hunger. However, as 'enlightened' consumers we will each have a particular favourite brand *that we have learned to value* above another. Here is our motivation to buy.

This investment of value means that the choice between brands is no longer trivial. It *does* matter which tin of beans we purchase, which pair of jeans we wear or which fizzy drink we consume. It matters to the extent that "we wouldn't be seen dead" wearing brand-X and in some cases, we would[15].

This 'added *value*' of a brand is the marketer's mantra but does it reside in the product itself? When we see the logo or brand name for Coca Cola or Mercedes (and you can see them now!), we associate far more than a fizzy drink or car with the product. It's young, it's freedom, it's about friendship or luxury, success, and being admired. These features are not an embodiment of the product, they are in our heads! They are part of our mental schema for each particular brand, which gives the brand its meaning. This mental representation contains propositions, imagery, sounds, smells, tastes and *emotional responses* based upon previous experiences of the brand.

Such psychological responses to the brands are automatic. We cannot deny them and more worryingly, they are

---

[15] "Their criminality is driven by a hunger for 'objects of desire', mobile phones, trainers and designer clothes..." Ian Burell, The Independent, March 2002.

often occurring at a subconscious level[16]. This 'cloud of unknowing' which surrounds brands is what they *symbolize* to us. They obtain their distinctive value because of purely psychological qualities that we attribute to them.

It is worth mentioning here that a large part of our previous encounters with brands happen vicariously. We watch others' enjoy friendship, luxury or success as part of a marketing or advertising campaign. And we learn to associate satisfaction of these needs with the brand without being aware of the learning taking place[17]. Very Freudian!

Now all this might not matter much if the brands delivered what they promised. It is clear that one brand of fizzy drink will quench our thirst as well as another or any brand of baked beans will serve to satiate our hunger. There is no problem with the linkage between physical products and their ability to satisfy *physiological needs*. However, the connection between products and their capacity to gratify *psychological needs* is tenuous and deceitful. How can 'things' from the material world possibly have a real and lasting impact on our mental and spiritual lives?

Which brand are we going to buy to show friendship? How do we purchase love? How much are we going to

[16] Coke reaches parts of the brain that other brands don't reach! Montague, P. R., 2004, Baylor College, Houston.

[17] Complete the phrase: "A Mars a day helps you...." Now how did you learn that?

acquire 'to be somebody'? What gift are we going to present ourselves with to find a meaning in life?

It is depressing to realise that most of us at some time in our lives try to pay money for all these 'things', using the currency of brands and their associated symbolic sugary coating. This psychological sweetener is like the bloom of a pink candyfloss. It promises everlasting joy and satisfaction but with one bite it withers and melts away. Want another? Want something new; a bigger and better one; a different colour perhaps? Why not buy two?

This is the cycle of psychological dissatisfaction that is stimulating runaway consumption and in turn feeding energy-hungry factories. Depletion of fuel reserves, despoliation of the environment and pollution follow in harmony with this deadly tango between Freud and Ford.

We are chasing happiness and spiritual fulfilment using a twisted map. What we value has been rerouted by branding. Like children, we believe in their fairy tales. Welcome to the kindergarten! Welcome to the candyfloss culture!

9

Empirical Experiment:

Colour and gender differences

It was hypothesised that the study will examine that colour affects the way we think, behave in an environment. We as individuals find colour combinations build mixed feelings (e.g. pleasant and dull). It is often believed that colour says a "lot" about one's personality. Our senses also play in accordance (smell, noise etc.); and finally colour is much more noticeable than objects within a place or setting.

The objective of the empirical study was to examine how specific colour interiors affect the why we behave and feel in various ways when placed in a work environment. The study explored the importance of colour and interior design, whilst establishing and developing individual awareness through careful application of colour. It provided a comprehensive understanding of colour and emotions. The study addressed the effects of colour on human emotions.

Twenty participants were used in order to conduct a pilot study, which offered a basis of what was expected, participants were recruited from London Metropolitan University (range from Undergraduates and Postgraduate students). Once the pilot study was completed, there was a need for a second empirical study to be carried amongst forty participants.

As the pilot study indicated levels of arousal and with the change of colour applications I would receive exactly the responses I would need to prove in relation to the question that colours really impact the environment and us. Once again, forty participants were recruited from London Metropolitan University.

For the experiment to be carried out the following tools were used: Microsoft PowerPoint slides containing 4 images; questionnaires produced in paper format to each participant; and pencils provided to participants to allocate their responses on the questionnaire.

The procedure that was involved to carry out this study was to ensure that the participants consented, and thus asked to sign a consent form; participants were then asked to read the instructions carefully; and finally the participants were told that each image on PowerPoint was timed 5 seconds, and then the page would go blank.

The design that was used to conduct this study was a between subjects analysis. The questionnaire was developed using a mixed design using quantitative and qualitative methods (See Figure 7.1).

Figure 7.1 illustrates an example of the questionnaire used to conduct this empirical study

INTRODUCTION
This is an investigation about office interiors.
It involves a series of 4 pictures that will be presented to you after another.

INSTRUCTIONS
Please read the following instruction before you begin the test.

1. The pictures that will appear on the screen are of office interiors.
2. You have 5 seconds to look at the image.
3. You will then be asked to immediately describe your feelings about the room using the scales below.
4. Overall there will be four images presented to you and we would like your responses to each one.

Thank you for taking the time to help with this study.

☐ Male
☐ Female

Please indicate your response after you have viewed IMAGE 1.

What are your impressions of Image 1?
Please indicate your response by allocating 1 as the lowest and 5 as the hightest.

Emotional	1	2	3	4	5
Active	1	2	3	4	5
Enjoyable	1	2	3	4	5
Charming	1	2	3	4	5
Quiet	1	2	3	4	5
Stimulating	1	2	3	4	5
Refined	1	2	3	4	5
Encouraging	1	2	3	4	5
Exciting	1	2	3	4	5
Boring	1	2	3	4	5
Interesting	1	2	3	4	5
Uncomfortable	1	2	3	4	5

What is your overall feeling of office 1?
_____
_____

The study used both qualitative and quantitative designs; the quantitative research dealt with the quantities of variables that involve the measurement of quantity or amount of the responses allocated by each participant. Whilst the qualitative research offered a more subjective response that was made up in a written style, and do not involve any statistical measure. So, why conduct a mix design? Simple, really, the designed offered numerical measures and in depth analysis, which proved successful.

Two measures were introduced to this study: the first stage involved a pilot study, which was conducted among twenty London Metropolitan University students. There were equal numbers of males and females. The questionnaire used to carry out this experiment used a five-point Likert scale in paper format and PowerPoint slides as each image was timed 5 seconds.

The second stage involved a study to be carried out among forty London Metropolitan University students; once again, the same questionnaire design was applied. The basis for the pilot study was to give a prediction of what was expected, how successful or not.

The experiment was conducted in a prestigious ICT lab; which meant all twenty subjects could participate in the pilot stage at the same time; further it also equipped all forty subjects to participate in the second study of the experiment.

Once the pilot study was completed the data was analysed using Univariate Analysis as this allowed to explore each variable in a data set separately. The Univariate Analysis looks at the range of values as well as the central tendency of the values. It produces a pattern of responses to the variable, whilst describing each variable on its own merit.

The second analyses of data were made using Tests Between Subjects Effects (ANOVA); where the Independent variables were: Gender and Image. Thus, the dependent variables were: Emotional, Active, Enjoyable, Charming, Quiet, Stimulating, Refined, Encouraging, Exciting, Boring, Interesting, and Uncomfortable.

It is therefore worth bearing in mind that the data analyses were made using Descriptives (Group Statistics) and Independent Samples T-test.

The results were then derived from the data analysed; figure 7.2 illustrates the results using Profile plots, and as can be seen, the Estimated Marginal means for each variable. For example, the results for **Emotional**, according to the Profile Plots, females found Image 1 and 3 far more **Emotional** than compared to males. In comparison, however males found Image 2 **Emotional.**

Nonetheless, both males and females found Image 4 equally **Emotional.** As can be viewed, there was not necessarily any significance found for Dependent variables: Emotional; as mentioned vaguely, additionally as no significance found for the following variables: Active, Enjoyable, Charming, Quiet, Stimulating, Refined, Encouraging, Exciting, Boring, Interesting and Uncomfortable.

However the analysis made from the pilot study describes each variable; for instance dependent variable **Active,** indicates that males scored incredibly high for image 2 whilst females scored slightly higher then males for image 3 and 4. For dependent variable **Enjoyable,** both males and females scored equally high for image 1, however, males scored relatively high for image 2 and 4 where as females scored high for image 3.

The fourth dependent variable is **Charming,** as seen in the Profile Plots, females scored higher for image 1 and 3 whilst males scored high for image and 2 and 4. The fifth dependent variable is **Quiet,** indicates that females scored higher for image 1 and 2, whereas, males scored higher for image 3 and 4. The sixth variable is **Stimulating,** and as shown in the Profile Plots, females found image 1 and 3 much more stimulating, than compared to males, however, males found image 2 and 4 slightly more stimulating. It is worth noting, the seventh dependent variable **Refined,** indicates that males found all images (1,2,3,4) slightly more refined, whilst females scored low for all images (1,2,3,4). The eighth dependent variable **Encouraging,** males scored higher for image 1,2 and 4 whilst females scored higher for image 3.

The ninth dependent variable **Exciting,** both males and females found image 2 to be equally **Exciting,** however, males scored higher for image 4, whilst females scored higher for image 1 and 3. The tenth dependent variable **Boring,** a consistent result, females scored slightly higher for image 1 and 2 whilst males scored higher for image 3 and 4.

The eleventh variable **Interesting,** males found image 1,2 and 4 to be most **Interesting,** whilst females found image 3 to be most **Interesting.** The final dependent variable is **Uncomfortable,** illustrates that both males and females found image 4 equally **Uncomfortable,** however, males scored higher for image 2 and 3 whilst females found image 1 most **Uncomfortable.**

Figure 7.2 illustrates the results derived from the pilot study among twenty London Metropolitan University students

Profile Plots:

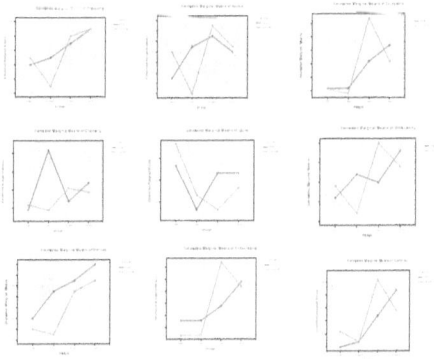

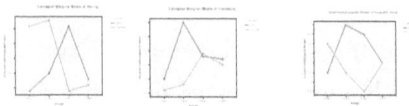

The results in figure 7.2 illustrate the profile plots for each variable, as can be seen; the pilot study was conducted using 4 images with two colour combination interiors; this measured the level of arousal the participant felt when he/or/she viewed the images; each image were timed 5 seconds, until the page went blank, which allowed the participant to allocate their response and any comments which was presented in a qualitative format.

Figure 7.3 illustrates all four images used in the pilot study; each image contain two colour combination interiors

Figure 7.4 illustrates all four images used in the second study; each image contain two colour combination interiors

Figure 7.5 illustrates the results derived from the data analysed using Independent T-tests (Group statistics). However, there were no such significant differences. Although responses collected qualitatively were much more positive.

Figure 7.5 illustrates the results of the second study; data collected and analysed using T-tests and Group statistics

Dependent variables	Male Mean (SD)	Female Mean (SD)
Emotional	2.34 (1.01)	2.31(1.01)
Active	2.48(1.16)	2.48(1.05)
Enjoyable	2.55(1.04)	2.62(1.20)
Charming	2.31(1.03)	2.45(1.17)
Quiet	2.96(1.67)	2.47(1.17)
Stimulating	2.66(1.18)	2.66(1.29)
Refined	2.76(1.17)	2.44(1.13)
Encouraging	2.22(1.17)	2.48(1.14)
Exciting	2.36(1.08)	2.37(1.22)
Boring	2.32(1.18)	2.28(1.36)
Interesting	2.31(1.14)	2.86(3.85)
Uncomfortable	2.32(1.27)	2.06(1.11)

Note: Results collected from Independent Samples T- test. Significance indicated for dependent variable Quiet ($t=2.18$, $df=158$ $p<0.05$) and dependent variable Refined ($t=1.752$, $df=158$ $p<0.05$)

-Without a single doubt, this book offers chapters beyond excitement; quite frankly the chapters have been designed in the way to offer you an insight that classical psychology, philosophy all has its creative flare. How you apply it remains your decision-

-Reena Begum-

2007

www.ingramcontent.com/pod-product-compliance
Lightning Source LLC
Chambersburg PA
CBHW031249280526
45784CB00004B/1784